MathFlare

Name: ______________________________

Class: ____________

Teacher: ______________________________

<u>Introduction</u>

As parents and educators, we recognize the pivotal role mathematics plays in shaping a child's academic journey and future success. Yet, the path to mathematical proficiency can often seem daunting, fraught with challenges and complexities. That's where the transformative power of MathFlare Workbooks shine through, illuminating the way forward with clarity, precision, and purpose.

Introducing MathFlare Workbooks – a beacon of guidance, a testament to excellence, and a catalyst for achievement. Crafted with meticulous care and expertise, MathFlare Workbooks stand as paragons of educational excellence, designed to nurture young minds, ignite a passion for learning, and develop a deep-rooted understanding of mathematical concepts.

Picture this: your child eagerly delves into the pages of Mathflare Workbook, greeted by a step-by-step guide illuminated with vivid examples that demystify complex mathematical concepts. With each turn of the page, they embark on a journey of discovery, encountering thoughtfully curated practice questions that reinforce learning and hone problem-solving skills. And when they unveil the answers to those very questions, a sense of accomplishment blossoms within them – a tangible reward for their hard work and dedication.

But MathFlare Workbooks are more than just tools for learning; they are pathways to comprehension, fostering a deep-seated understanding of mathematical concepts through a sequential, logical flow. From fundamental principles to advanced problem-solving strategies, every chapter builds upon the last, ensuring a robust foundation upon which future knowledge can be constructed.

As parents, we yearn for nothing more than to see our children thrive, to witness the spark of inspiration ignited within them as they conquer academic challenges with confidence and poise. MathFlare Workbooks serve as partners in this noble endeavor, offering not just practice questions, but the keys to unlocking a world of opportunity.

And for teachers, MathFlare Workbooks stand as invaluable allies in the quest to cultivate mathematical proficiency in the classroom. With answers readily available, instructors can focus on guiding and nurturing their students, confident in the knowledge that MathFlare Workbooks provide a solid framework upon which to build.

In the pages of MathFlare Workbooks, we find not just the promise of academic excellence, but the seeds of a brighter tomorrow. So let us embrace the power of mathematics, let us champion the journey of learning, and let us pave the way for a generation of young minds poised to shape the world. With MathFlare Workbooks as our guide, the possibilities are infinite, and the future, bright.

Table of Contents

MathFlare
Grade 5
MATH WORKBOOK
Step by Step Guide and Essential Practice with Answers
Multiplication Division
Place Value and Expanded Notations
Fractions and Geometry
Unit Conversion
MathFlare Publishing

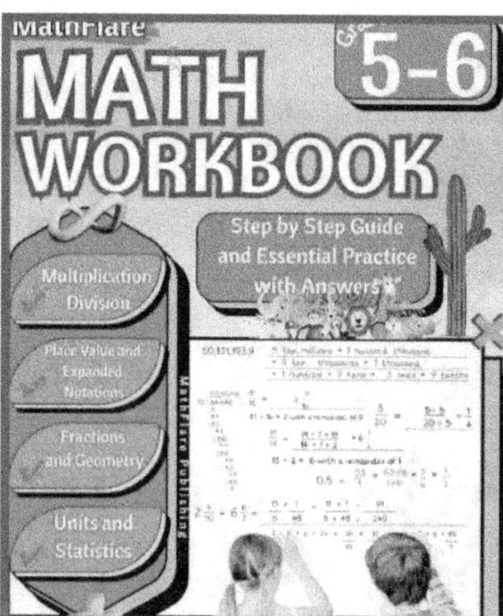

MathFlare
Grade 5-6
MATH WORKBOOK
Step by Step Guide and Essential Practice with Answers
Multiplication Division
Place Value and Expanded Notations
Fractions and Geometry
Units and Statistics
MathFlare Publishing

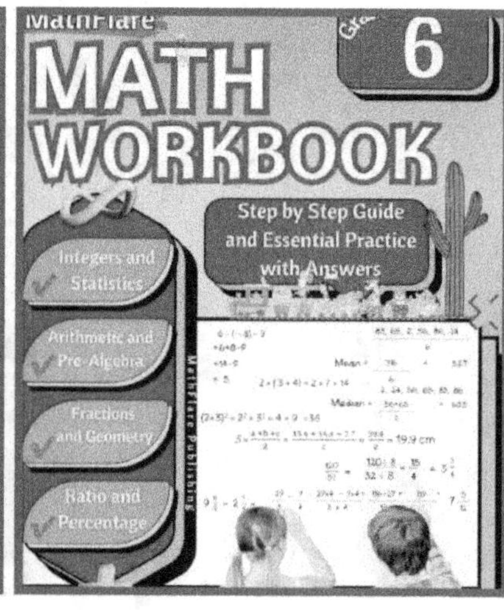

MathFlare
Grade 6
MATH WORKBOOK
Step by Step Guide and Essential Practice with Answers
Integers and Statistics
Arithmetic and Pre-Algebra
Fractions and Geometry
Ratio and Percentage
MathFlare Publishing

MathFlare
Grade 6-7
MATH WORKBOOK
Step by Step Guide and Essential Practice with Answers
Arithmetic and Pre-Algebra
Ratio, Percent Proportion
Geometry
Statistics
MathFlare Publishing

MathFlare
Grade 7
MATH WORKBOOK
Step by Step Guide and Essential Practice with Answers
Pre-Algebra
Ratio, Percent Proportion
Geometry
Statistics
MathFlare Publishing

MathFlare
Grade 7-8
MATH WORKBOOK
Step by Step Guide and Essential Practice with Answers
Pre-Algebra
Ratio, Percent Proportion
Geometry and Cartesian Plane
Statistics
MathFlare Publishing

MathFlare
Grade 8-9
MATH WORKBOOK
Step by Step Guide and Essential Practice with Answers
Pre-Algebra
Ratio, Proportion and Percentage
Linear Equations
Geometry and Cartesian Plane
MathFlare Publishing

MathFlare
Grade 8
MATH WORKBOOK
Step by Step Guide and Essential Practice with Answers
Pre-Algebra
Percentage
Linear Equations
Geometry
MathFlare Publishing

Long Division

Division is like the opposite of multiplication. It's all about sharing or distributing items equally among a certain number of groups or people.

When we divide one number by another, we're essentially splitting a number into equal parts. We're figuring out how many groups of a certain size can be made from that number.

For instance, let's divide 20 by 4.

When we divide 20 by 4, we're essentially asking, "How many groups of size 4 can we make from 20?"

Now, there are several parts or terms involved in the division process:

- Dividend: This is the number being divided, which in this case, is 20.

- Divisor: This is the number we're dividing by, which is 4.

- Quotient: This is the answer we get after dividing. It tells us how many groups of the divisor can be made from the dividend. In this case, the answer is 5.

So, when we divide 20 by 4, we found out that 5 groups of 4 can be made from 20.

Let's solve problems from exercises:

$$
\begin{array}{r}
18 \\
2\overline{)36} \\
-2 \\
\hline
16 \\
-16 \\
\hline
0
\end{array}
\qquad
\begin{array}{r}
5 \\
2\overline{)10} \\
-10 \\
\hline
0
\end{array}
$$

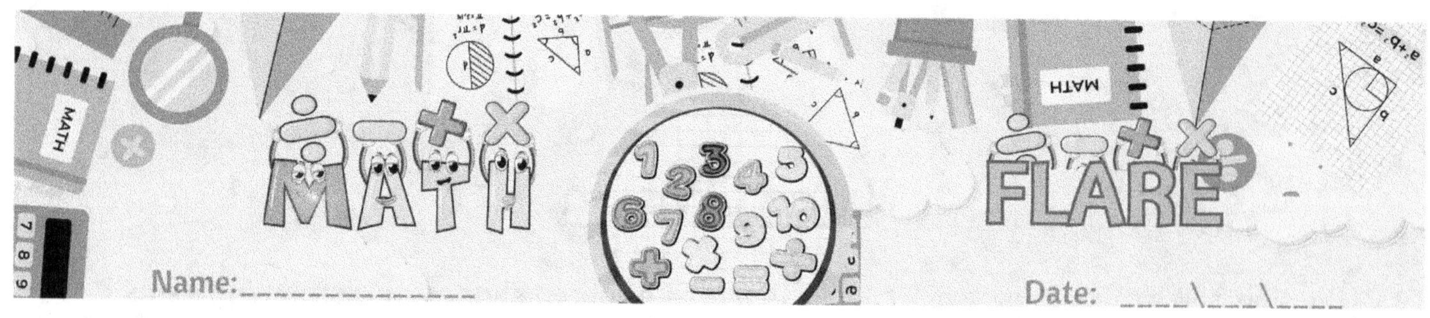

Basic Division

Find the quotient.

1.
$8\overline{)88}$

2.
$8\overline{)152}$

3.
$4\overline{)52}$

4.
$3\overline{)42}$

5.
$5\overline{)60}$

6.
$7\overline{)42}$

7.
$2\overline{)18}$

8.
$9\overline{)99}$

9.
$3\overline{)48}$

10.
$4\overline{)16}$

11.
$6\overline{)12}$

12.
$4\overline{)28}$

13.
$9\overline{)126}$

14.
$4\overline{)56}$

15.
$7\overline{)112}$

16.
$2\overline{)20}$

17. $8\overline{)48}$	18. $5\overline{)10}$	19. $2\overline{)30}$	20. $10\overline{)110}$
21. $5\overline{)90}$	22. $8\overline{)120}$	23. $5\overline{)15}$	24. $5\overline{)5}$
25. $2\overline{)6}$	26. $6\overline{)18}$	27. $6\overline{)90}$	28. $2\overline{)28}$
29. $4\overline{)44}$	30. $10\overline{)140}$	31. $5\overline{)25}$	32. $6\overline{)102}$

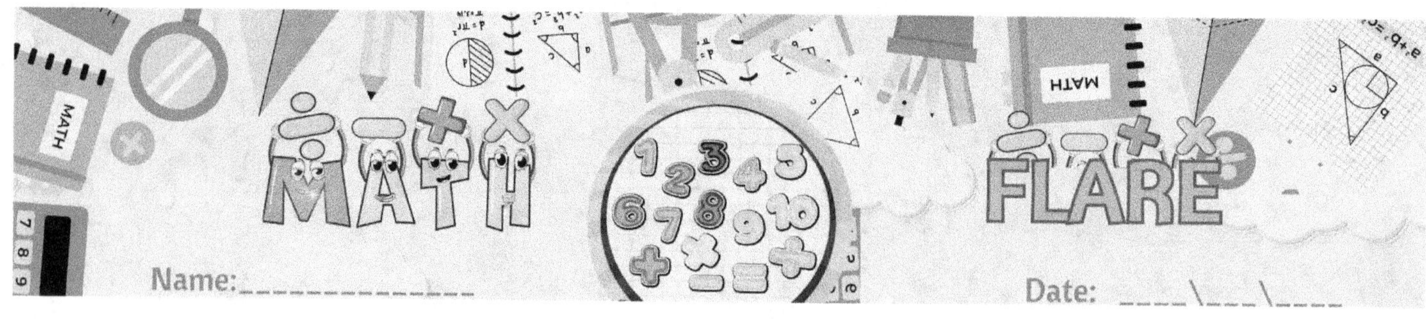

33.

$10\overline{)170}$

34.

$1\overline{)14}$

35.

$7\overline{)77}$

36.

$2\overline{)2}$

37.

$7\overline{)70}$

38.

$3\overline{)15}$

39.

$7\overline{)14}$

40.

$10\overline{)130}$

41.

$7\overline{)105}$

42.

$9\overline{)18}$

43.

$5\overline{)45}$

44.

$5\overline{)50}$

45.

$3\overline{)36}$

46.

$2\overline{)24}$

47.

$10\overline{)80}$

48.

$4\overline{)80}$

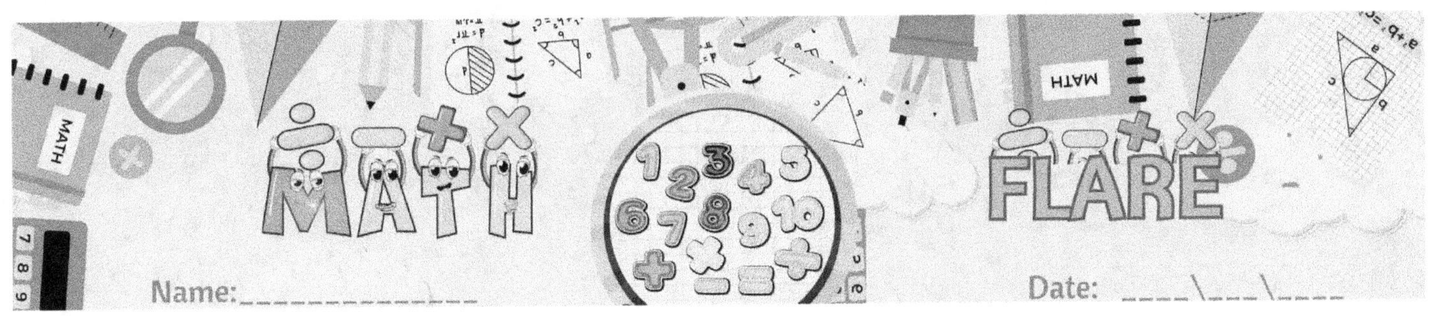

49.

$$9 \overline{)180}$$

50.

$$4 \overline{)24}$$

51.

$$3 \overline{)51}$$

52.

$$2 \overline{)12}$$

53.

$$9 \overline{)171}$$

54.

$$3 \overline{)21}$$

55.

$$1 \overline{)20}$$

56.

$$9 \overline{)117}$$

57.

$$7 \overline{)133}$$

58.

$$7 \overline{)35}$$

59.

$$3 \overline{)30}$$

60.

$$1 \overline{)8}$$

61.

$$3 \overline{)18}$$

62.

$$8 \overline{)16}$$

63.

$$4 \overline{)36}$$

64.

$$7 \overline{)7}$$

65.

9)54

66.

2)8

67.

7)126

68.

2)38

69.

7)98

70.

8)128

71.

4)60

72.

6)24

73.

3)57

74.

6)42

75.

5)55

76.

8)8

77.

4)8

78.

3)33

79.

3)24

80.

8)32

81. $7\overline{)119}$

82. $3\overline{)45}$

83. $5\overline{)20}$

84. $6\overline{)72}$

85. $3\overline{)39}$

86. $10\overline{)20}$

87. $5\overline{)80}$

88. $8\overline{)144}$

89. $7\overline{)28}$

90. $5\overline{)95}$

91. $9\overline{)153}$

92. $7\overline{)21}$

93. $9\overline{)135}$

94. $6\overline{)96}$

95. $2\overline{)26}$

96. $8\overline{)96}$

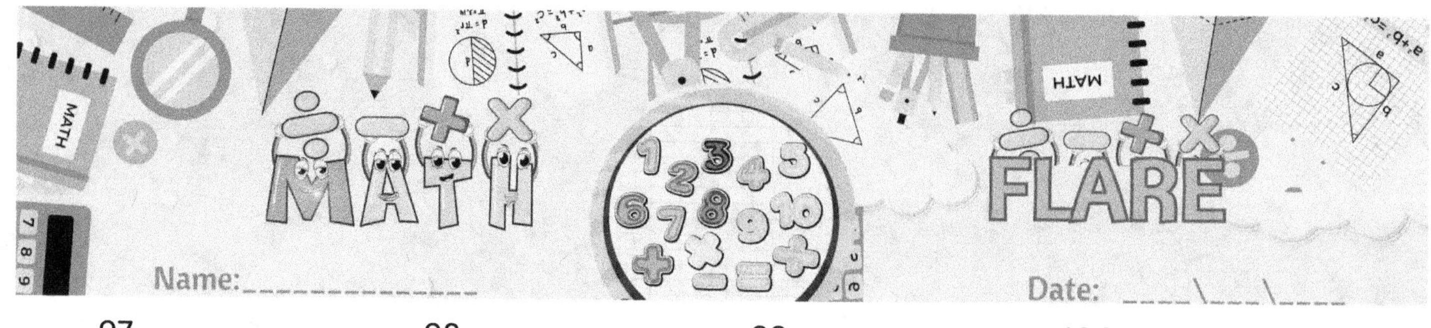

97. 5)85

98. 4)64

99. 5)65

100. 1)12

101. 8)64

102. 1)19

103. 9)90

104. 9)72

105. 9)108

106. 5)75

107. 1)15

108. 9)144

109. 10)60

110. 1)1

111. 4)68

112. 6)84

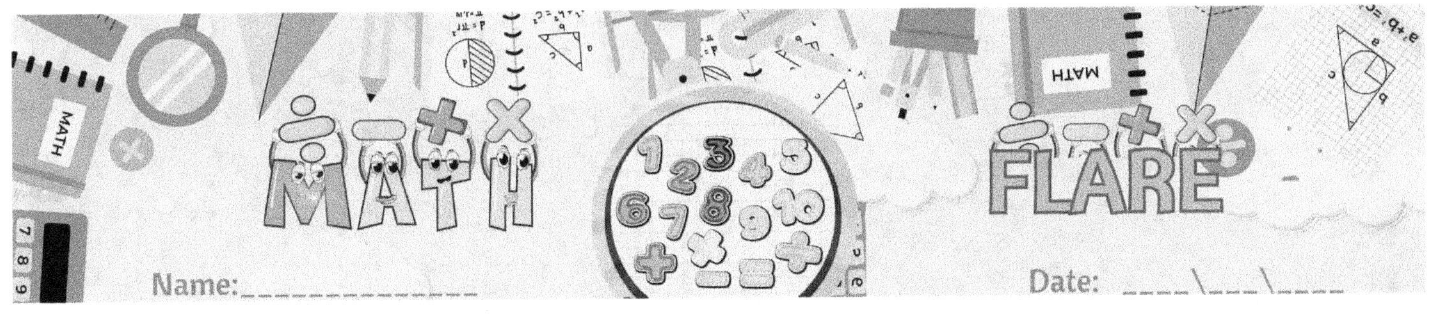

113.

$2\overline{)34}$

114.

$6\overline{)54}$

115.

$1\overline{)9}$

116.

$5\overline{)70}$

117.

$6\overline{)78}$

118.

$6\overline{)6}$

119.

$9\overline{)162}$

120.

$6\overline{)120}$

121.

$7\overline{)49}$

122.

$3\overline{)12}$

123.

$8\overline{)80}$

124.

$10\overline{)90}$

125.

$10\overline{)70}$

126.

$1\overline{)7}$

127.

$4\overline{)40}$

128.

$1\overline{)6}$

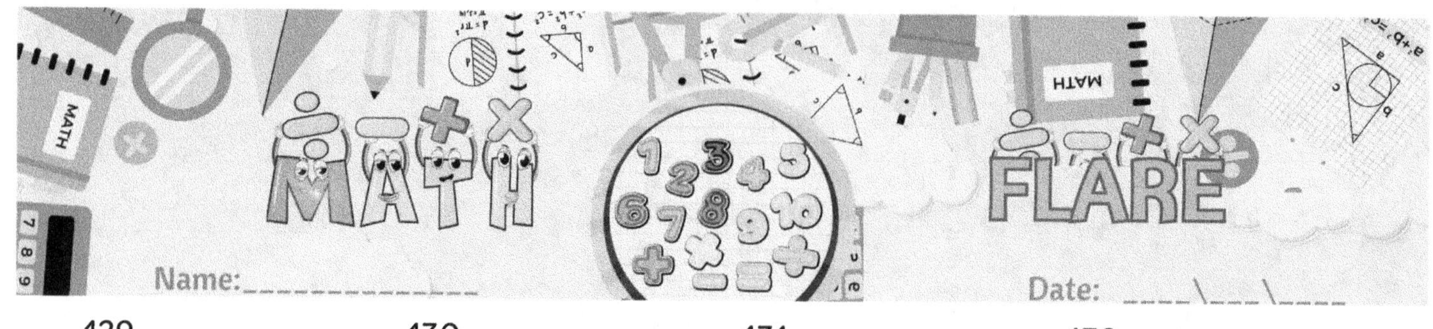

129. $3\overline{)27}$

130. $4\overline{)48}$

131. $6\overline{)36}$

132. $1\overline{)13}$

133. $6\overline{)48}$

134. $10\overline{)100}$

135. $4\overline{)12}$

136. $2\overline{)40}$

137. $6\overline{)60}$

138. $8\overline{)112}$

139. $9\overline{)36}$

140. $5\overline{)40}$

141. $3\overline{)54}$

142. $1\overline{)11}$

143. $6\overline{)66}$

144. $6\overline{)30}$

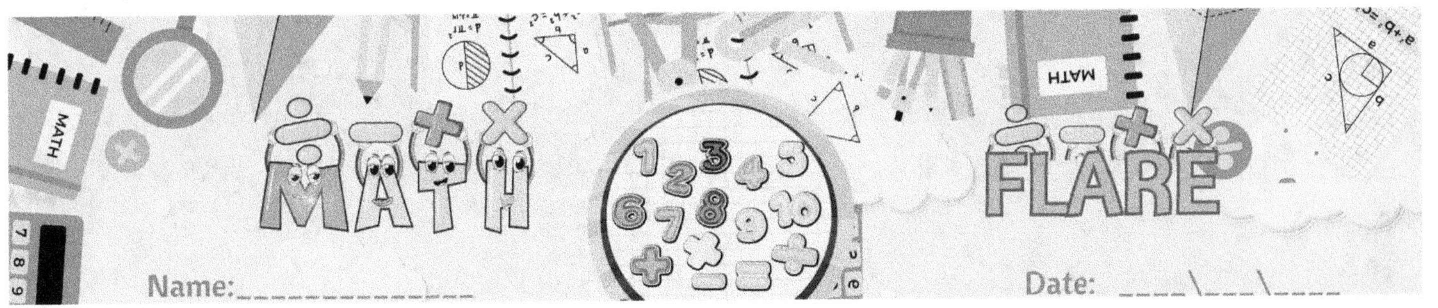

145. $1\overline{)17}$

146. $2\overline{)12}$

147. $8\overline{)96}$

148. $1\overline{)16}$

149. $8\overline{)112}$

150. $4\overline{)28}$

151. $9\overline{)36}$

152. $9\overline{)81}$

153. $3\overline{)39}$

154. $3\overline{)51}$

155. $6\overline{)24}$

156. $8\overline{)32}$

157. $2\overline{)28}$

158. $1\overline{)2}$

159. $10\overline{)160}$

160. $5\overline{)85}$

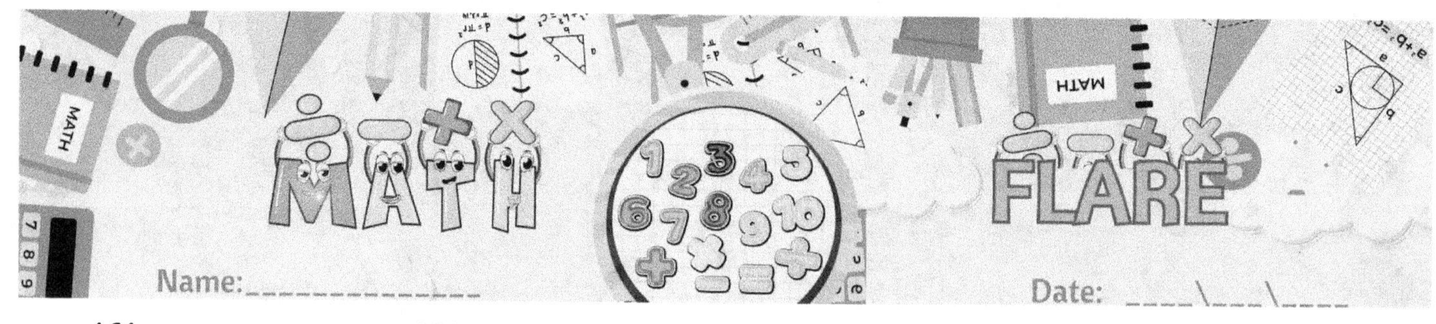

161. $9\overline{)54}$	162. $4\overline{)76}$	163. $1\overline{)3}$	164. $4\overline{)40}$
165. $8\overline{)144}$	166. $7\overline{)70}$	167. $9\overline{)45}$	168. $1\overline{)5}$
169. $10\overline{)170}$	170. $1\overline{)20}$	171. $3\overline{)9}$	172. $6\overline{)114}$
173. $8\overline{)8}$	174. $2\overline{)6}$	175. $9\overline{)18}$	176. $4\overline{)52}$

177.

8⟌24

178.

8⟌72

179.

9⟌171

180.

10⟌30

181.

4⟌44

182.

9⟌63

183.

2⟌10

184.

9⟌9

185.

3⟌24

186.

8⟌128

187.

6⟌18

188.

4⟌24

189.

7⟌35

190.

6⟌84

191.

7⟌21

192.

4⟌48

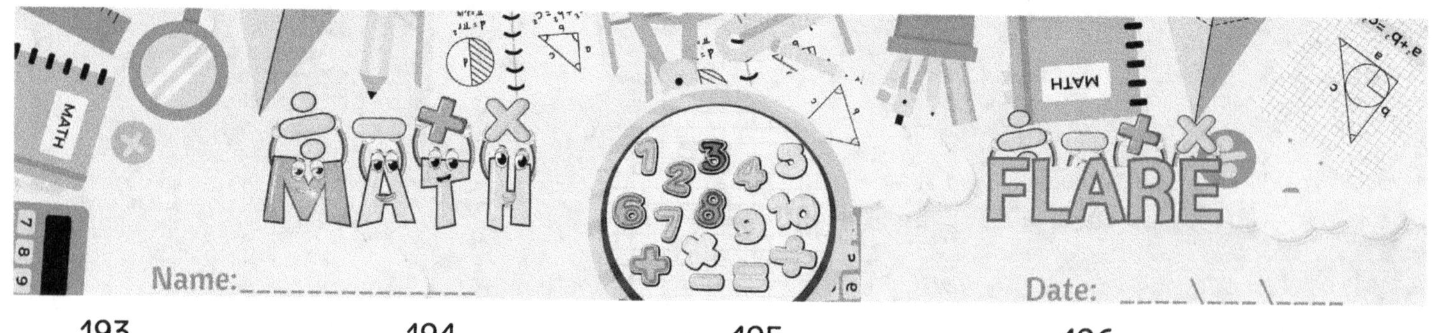

193.
$$5\overline{)90}$$

194.
$$5\overline{)60}$$

195.
$$9\overline{)27}$$

196.
$$3\overline{)36}$$

197.
$$2\overline{)18}$$

198.
$$6\overline{)42}$$

199.
$$2\overline{)34}$$

200.
$$10\overline{)150}$$

201.
$$3\overline{)18}$$

202.
$$5\overline{)70}$$

203.
$$5\overline{)100}$$

204.
$$2\overline{)26}$$

205.
$$1\overline{)6}$$

206.
$$6\overline{)36}$$

207.
$$2\overline{)14}$$

208.
$$8\overline{)48}$$

209.	210.	211.	212.
3)‾12	7)‾28	5)‾40	7)‾98

213.	214.	215.	216.
4)‾60	5)‾30	8)‾104	6)‾108

217.	218.	219.	220.
3)‾45	9)‾144	10)‾190	3)‾21

221.	222.	223.	224.
4)‾32	5)‾45	4)‾20	6)‾60

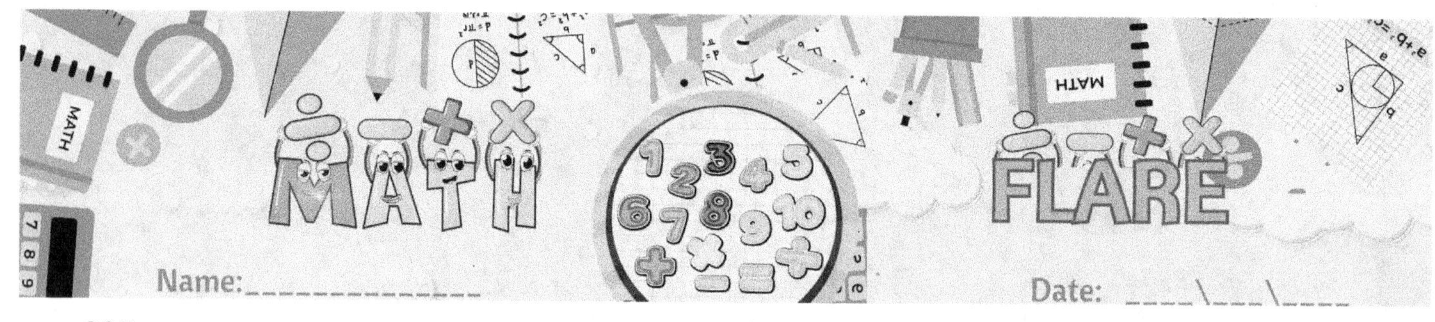

225.

3)30

226.

7)105

227.

8)80

228.

9)90

229.

9)108

230.

2)16

231.

2)32

232.

2)2

233.

6)48

234.

2)30

235.

8)120

236.

9)180

237.

1)19

238.

7)84

239.

2)4

240.

4)4

241.

10)50

242.

4)36

243.

10)180

244.

5)10

245.

10)100

246.

5)80

247.

4)16

248.

2)20

249.

1)18

250.

8)88

251.

6)96

252.

7)63

253.

10)130

254.

7)42

255.

8)40

256.

3)42

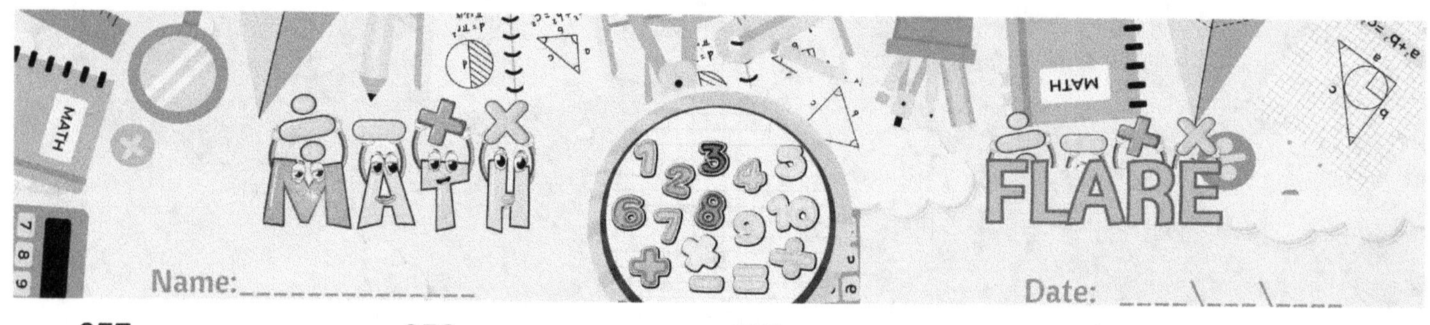

257.

$7\overline{)126}$

258.

$5\overline{)50}$

259.

$5\overline{)25}$

260.

$5\overline{)35}$

261.

$2\overline{)24}$

262.

$7\overline{)49}$

263.

$7\overline{)14}$

264.

$5\overline{)20}$

265.

$3\overline{)54}$

266.

$3\overline{)33}$

267.

$6\overline{)12}$

268.

$3\overline{)27}$

269.

$4\overline{)72}$

270.

$3\overline{)15}$

271.

$1\overline{)11}$

272.

$8\overline{)160}$

273.
$$7\overline{)7}$$

274.
$$6\overline{)72}$$

275.
$$3\overline{)57}$$

276.
$$1\overline{)12}$$

277.
$$6\overline{)90}$$

278.
$$5\overline{)95}$$

279.
$$3\overline{)60}$$

280.
$$9\overline{)99}$$

281.
$$5\overline{)65}$$

282.
$$7\overline{)119}$$

283.
$$2\overline{)36}$$

284.
$$2\overline{)8}$$

285.
$$2\overline{)22}$$

286.
$$3\overline{)6}$$

287.
$$4\overline{)56}$$

288.
$$8\overline{)64}$$

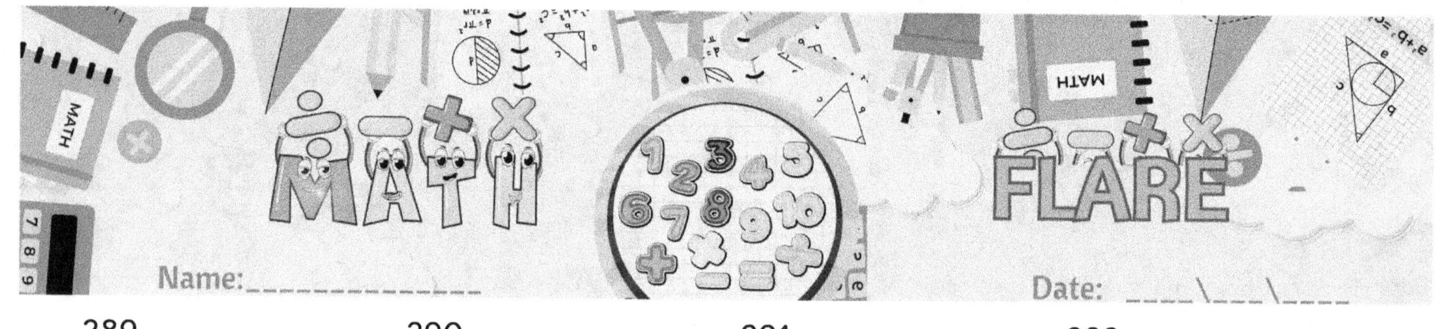

289.

$10\overline{)200}$

290.

$10\overline{)20}$

291.

$8\overline{)136}$

292.

$8\overline{)152}$

293.

$10\overline{)80}$

294.

$9\overline{)162}$

295.

$6\overline{)54}$

296.

$4\overline{)12}$

297.

$4\overline{)64}$

298.

$7\overline{)91}$

299.

$10\overline{)10}$

300.

$7\overline{)133}$

301.

$5\overline{)55}$

302.

$6\overline{)30}$

303.

$10\overline{)70}$

304.

$9\overline{)135}$

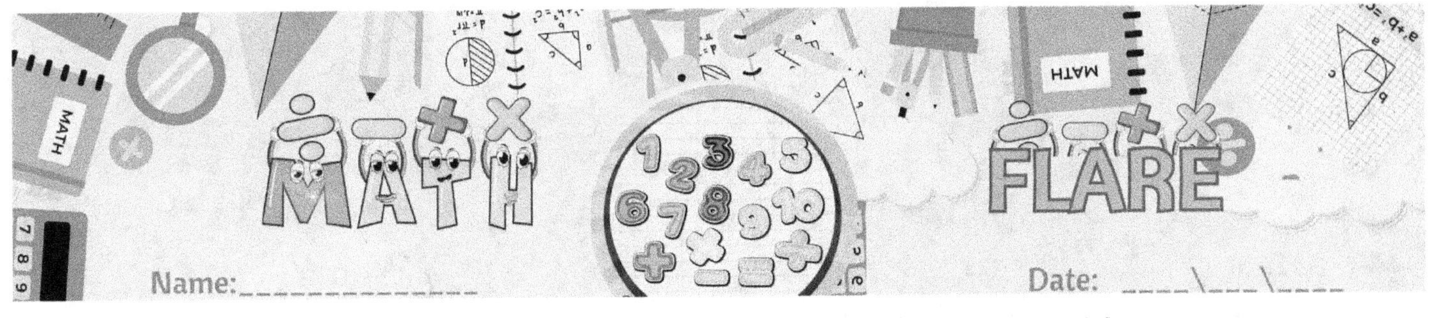

305.

$6\overline{)66}$

306.

$4\overline{)8}$

307.

$7\overline{)56}$

308.

$7\overline{)140}$

309.

$5\overline{)5}$

310.

$1\overline{)15}$

311.

$1\overline{)8}$

312.

$6\overline{)102}$

313.

$10\overline{)40}$

314.

$1\overline{)1}$

315.

$7\overline{)112}$

316.

$2\overline{)38}$

317.

$5\overline{)75}$

318.

$1\overline{)10}$

319.

$9\overline{)72}$

320.

$8\overline{)56}$

321. $4\overline{)68}$	322. $1\overline{)4}$	323. $10\overline{)60}$	324. $3\overline{)3}$
325. $10\overline{)140}$	326. $10\overline{)90}$	327. $8\overline{)16}$	328. $6\overline{)78}$
329. $5\overline{)15}$	330. $2\overline{)40}$	331. $7\overline{)77}$	332. $6\overline{)120}$
333. $1\overline{)13}$	334. $9\overline{)153}$	335. $1\overline{)9}$	336. $3\overline{)48}$

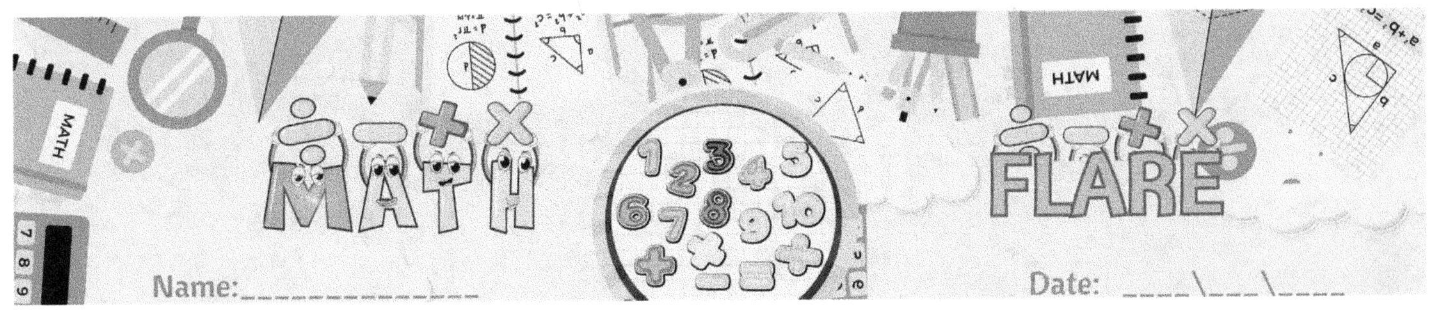

Name:_______________________   Date: ____________

Long Division

Find the quotient.

337.
$$7 \overline{)259}$$

338.
$$7 \overline{)630}$$

339.
$$6 \overline{)402}$$

340.
$$3 \overline{)117}$$

341.
$$5 \overline{)50}$$

342.
$$2 \overline{)144}$$

343.
$$6 \overline{)372}$$

344.
$$3 \overline{)240}$$

345.
$$7 \overline{)154}$$

346.
$$5 \overline{)100}$$

347.
$$5 \overline{)155}$$

348.
$$7 \overline{)553}$$

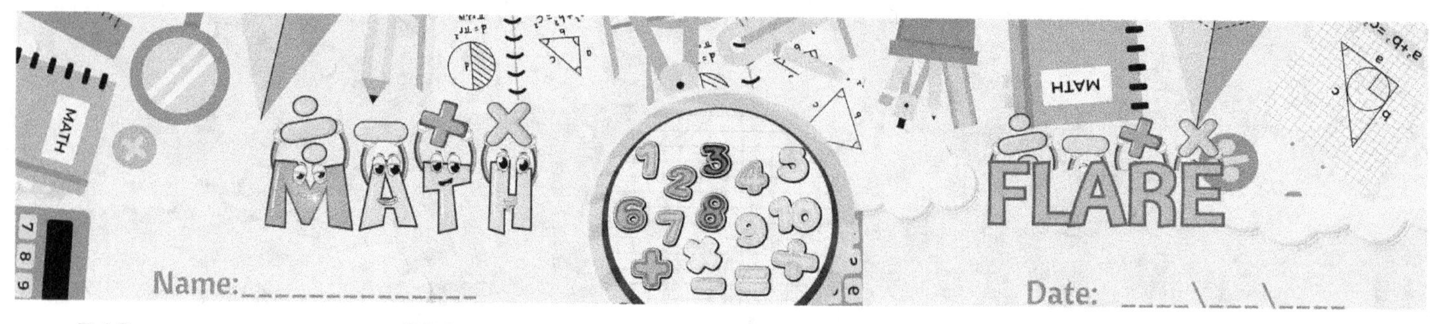

349.

3)207

350.

5)475

351.

3)267

352.

8)208

353.

7)665

354.

8)168

355.

6)516

356.

4)308

357.

7)301

358.

6)522

359.

2)50

360.

6)120

361.

9)738

362.

10)80

363.

4)128

364.

7)581

365.

7)574

366.

3)96

367.

3)162

368.

3)258

369.

1)60

370.

9)18

371.

3)243

372.

9)657

373.

5)40

374.

8)664

375.

7)686

376.

2)62

377.

4)316

378.

1)99

379.

4)248

380.

7)315

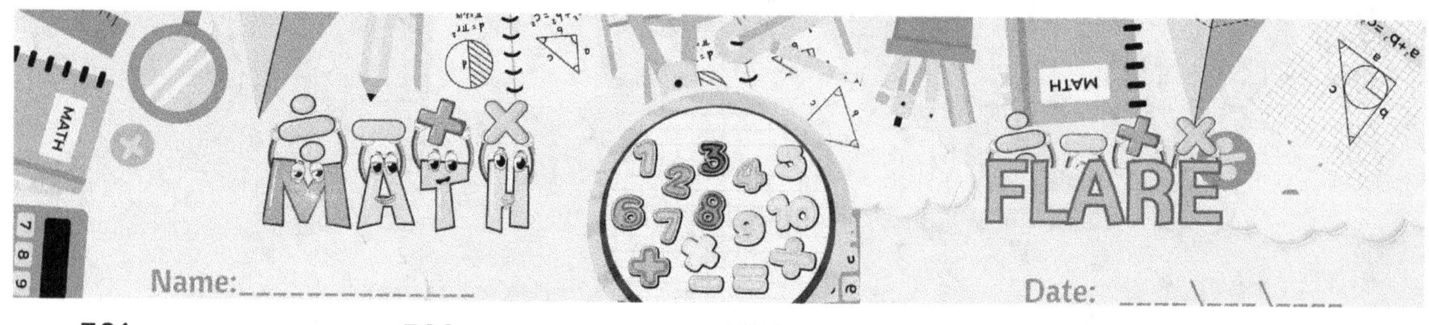

381. 6)438

382. 3)147

383. 6)234

384. 3)15

385. 6)132

386. 3)285

387. 4)256

388. 3)24

389. 9)207

390. 6)510

391. 2)140

392. 7)616

393. 1)39

394. 6)174

395. 6)246

396. 9)387

397.
$5\overline{)255}$

398.
$2\overline{)24}$

399.
$8\overline{)552}$

400.
$3\overline{)156}$

401.
$10\overline{)670}$

402.
$6\overline{)576}$

403.
$2\overline{)18}$

404.
$1\overline{)45}$

405.
$9\overline{)612}$

406.
$7\overline{)343}$

407.
$8\overline{)568}$

408.
$4\overline{)348}$

409.
$6\overline{)186}$

410.
$1\overline{)89}$

411.
$2\overline{)138}$

412.
$5\overline{)250}$

413. 2)94

414. 5)450

415. 7)420

416. 9)432

417. 9)324

418. 8)448

419. 3)144

420. 4)196

421. 6)486

422. 9)126

423. 6)258

424. 8)760

425. 2)186

426. 9)846

427. 3)30

428. 6)546

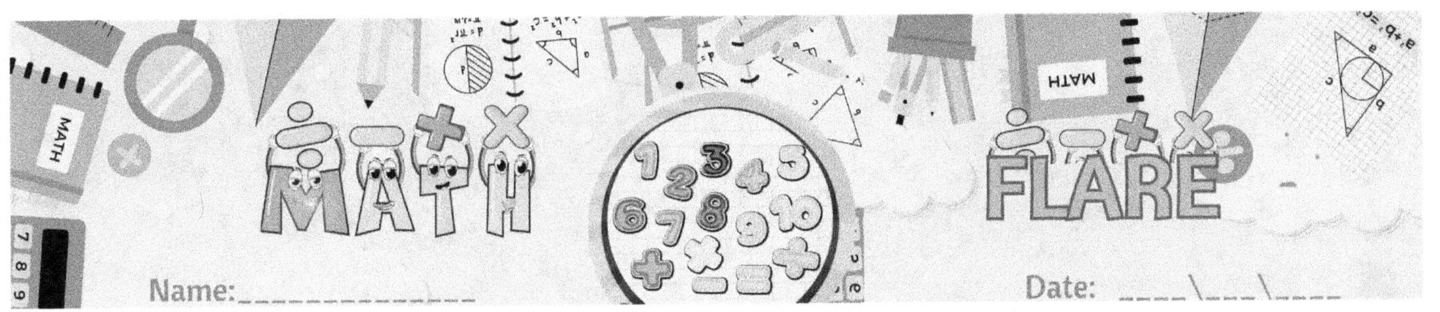

429.

$$6 \overline{)360}$$

430.

$$10 \overline{)570}$$

431.

$$1 \overline{)96}$$

432.

$$2 \overline{)6}$$

433.

$$6 \overline{)204}$$

434.

$$8 \overline{)24}$$

435.

$$2 \overline{)194}$$

436.

$$2 \overline{)38}$$

437.

$$5 \overline{)265}$$

438.

$$4 \overline{)136}$$

439.

$$8 \overline{)264}$$

440.

$$9 \overline{)594}$$

441.

$$8 \overline{)360}$$

442.

$$8 \overline{)8}$$

443.

$$4 \overline{)324}$$

444.

$$9 \overline{)792}$$

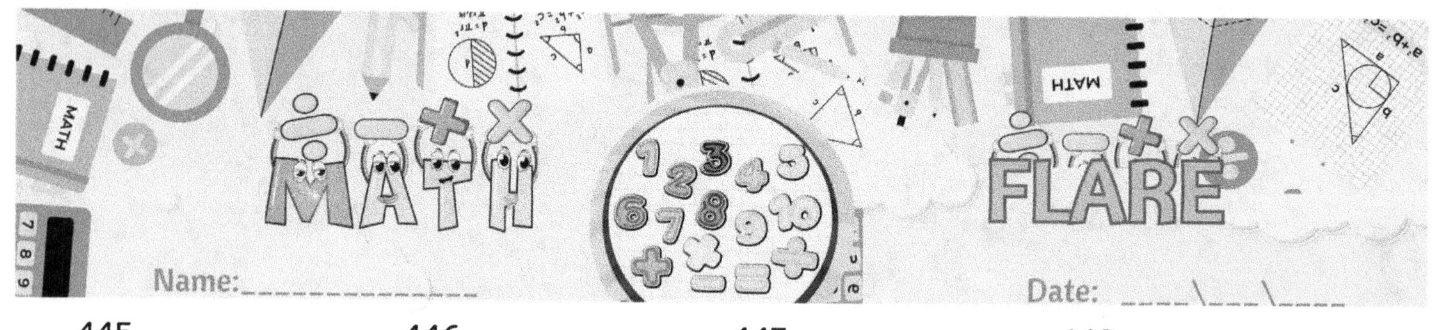

445.

$$1\overline{)61}$$

446.

$$5\overline{)400}$$

447.

$$5\overline{)310}$$

448.

$$8\overline{)688}$$

449.

$$6\overline{)168}$$

450.

$$7\overline{)504}$$

451.

$$9\overline{)171}$$

452.

$$8\overline{)544}$$

453.

$$5\overline{)330}$$

454.

$$8\overline{)144}$$

455.

$$7\overline{)245}$$

456.

$$9\overline{)549}$$

457.

$$3\overline{)114}$$

458.

$$4\overline{)220}$$

459.

$$1\overline{)1}$$

460.

$$3\overline{)66}$$

461.

9⟌459

462.

7⟌455

463.

2⟌142

464.

6⟌564

465.

8⟌496

466.

1⟌2

467.

6⟌342

468.

9⟌72

469.

6⟌384

470.

1⟌66

471.

8⟌696

472.

9⟌135

473.

10⟌830

474.

5⟌195

475.

6⟌30

476.

3⟌183

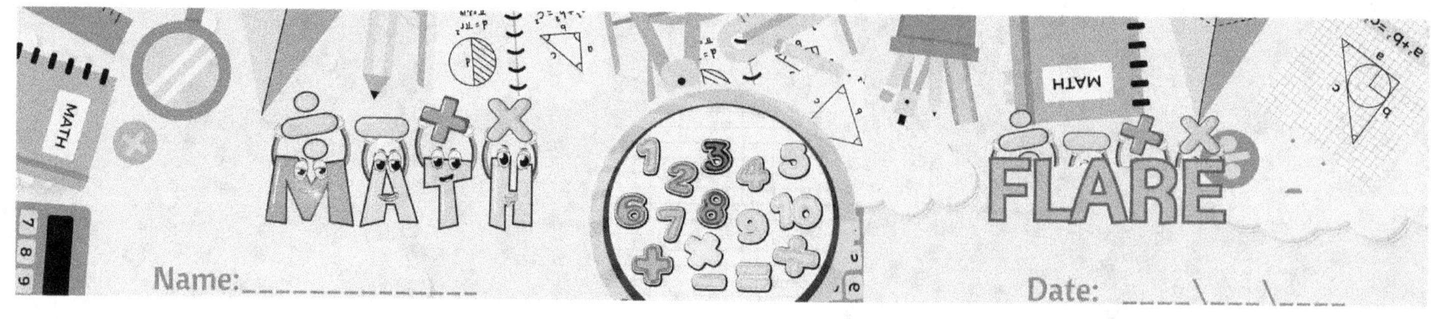

477.

$6\overline{)396}$

478.

$10\overline{)850}$

479.

$6\overline{)42}$

480.

$6\overline{)102}$

481.

$4\overline{)336}$

482.

$1\overline{)65}$

483.

$1\overline{)41}$

484.

$10\overline{)530}$

485.

$5\overline{)35}$

486.

$7\overline{)189}$

487.

$4\overline{)84}$

488.

$4\overline{)280}$

489.

$5\overline{)220}$

490.

$5\overline{)460}$

491.

$4\overline{)224}$

492.

$2\overline{)132}$

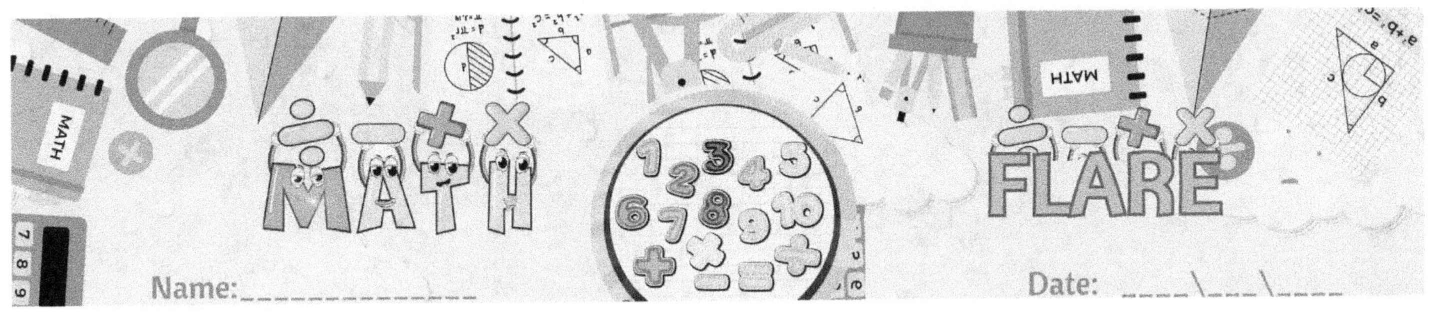

493.

$2\overline{)196}$

494.

$2\overline{)124}$

495.

$5\overline{)405}$

496.

$8\overline{)600}$

497.

$9\overline{)342}$

498.

$1\overline{)82}$

499.

$7\overline{)14}$

500.

$3\overline{)63}$

501.

$7\overline{)287}$

502.

$3\overline{)93}$

503.

$8\overline{)312}$

504.

$7\overline{)609}$

505.

$4\overline{)44}$

506.

$4\overline{)380}$

507.

$2\overline{)78}$

508.

$4\overline{)396}$

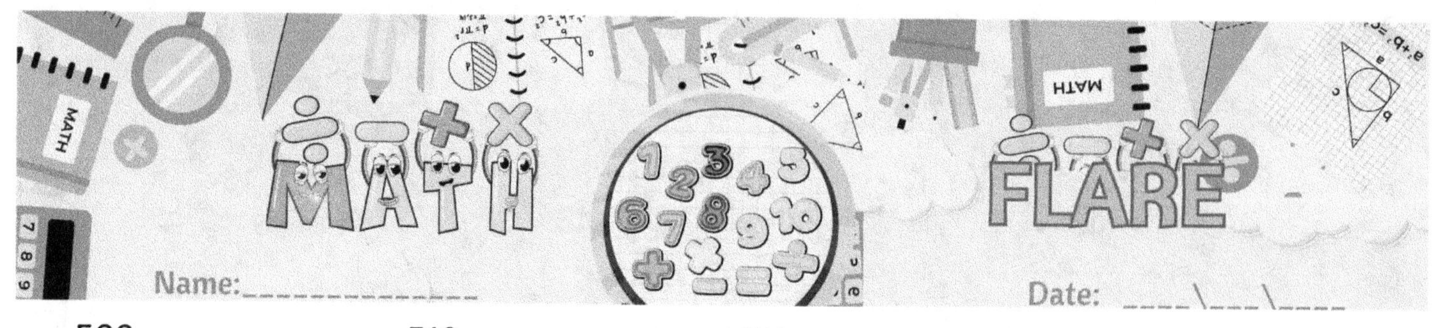

509.

$5 \overline{)410}$

510.

$7 \overline{)560}$

511.

$5 \overline{)280}$

512.

$4 \overline{)392}$

513.

$7 \overline{)406}$

514.

$8 \overline{)368}$

515.

$7 \overline{)77}$

516.

$9 \overline{)621}$

517.

$5 \overline{)390}$

518.

$3 \overline{)204}$

519.

$8 \overline{)560}$

520.

$5 \overline{)465}$

521.

$3 \overline{)186}$

522.

$6 \overline{)240}$

523.

$6 \overline{)552}$

524.

$7 \overline{)434}$

MathFlare - Long Division 2nd and 3rd Grade

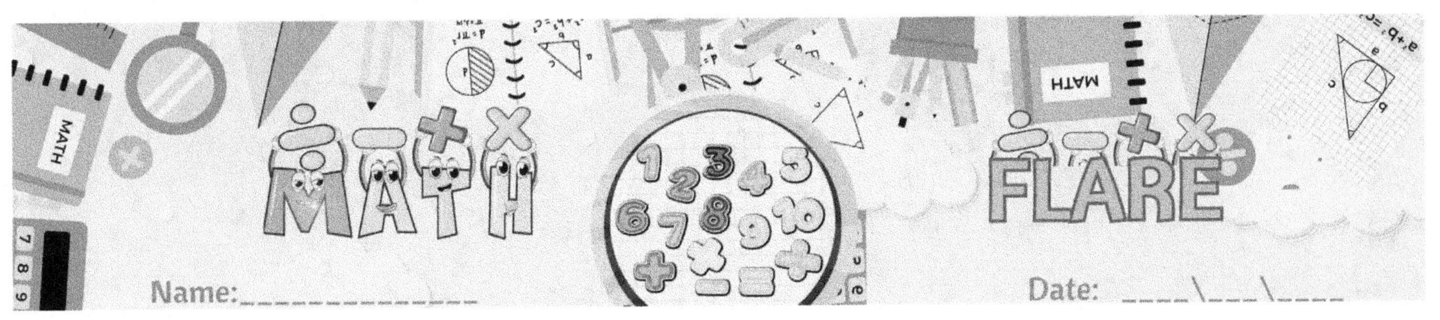

525. 9)198

526. 2)164

527. 1)13

528. 2)182

529. 5)125

530. 2)88

531. 9)495

532. 8)624

533. 1)95

534. 7)532

535. 8)608

536. 2)82

537. 5)180

538. 10)440

539. 9)558

540. 8)40

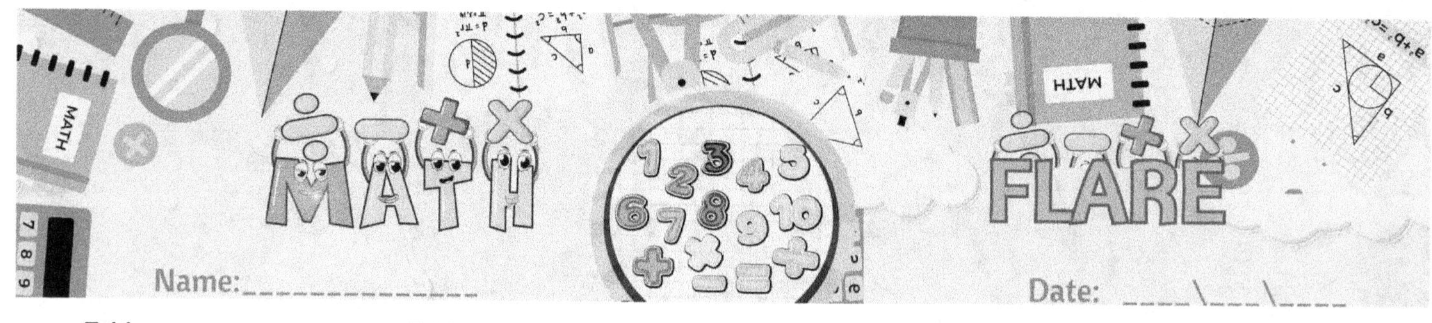

541.

$1 \overline{)1}$

542.

$4 \overline{)388}$

543.

$8 \overline{)552}$

544.

$4 \overline{)356}$

545.

$3 \overline{)162}$

546.

$3 \overline{)231}$

547.

$7 \overline{)21}$

548.

$3 \overline{)246}$

549.

$2 \overline{)24}$

550.

$1 \overline{)68}$

551.

$4 \overline{)84}$

552.

$7 \overline{)448}$

553.

$1 \overline{)78}$

554.

$7 \overline{)49}$

555.

$9 \overline{)162}$

556.

$2 \overline{)94}$

557. $2\overline{)112}$	558. $9\overline{)801}$	559. $3\overline{)216}$	560. $9\overline{)270}$
561. $6\overline{)174}$	562. $5\overline{)275}$	563. $7\overline{)623}$	564. $7\overline{)294}$
565. $2\overline{)34}$	566. $3\overline{)228}$	567. $6\overline{)78}$	568. $8\overline{)640}$
569. $4\overline{)264}$	570. $9\overline{)882}$	571. $2\overline{)48}$	572. $5\overline{)370}$

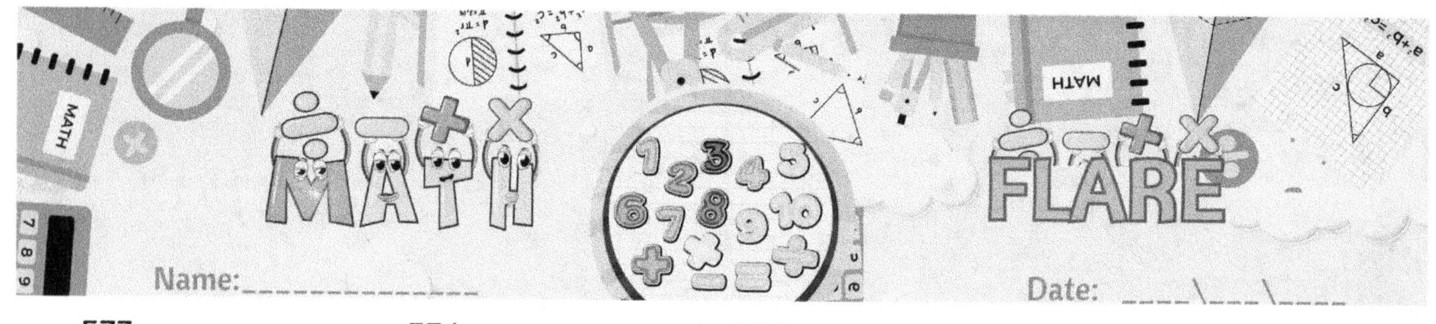

573. $7\overline{)84}$

574. $2\overline{)72}$

575. $6\overline{)270}$

576. $2\overline{)198}$

577. $8\overline{)120}$

578. $10\overline{)170}$

579. $2\overline{)44}$

580. $9\overline{)648}$

581. $9\overline{)351}$

582. $8\overline{)88}$

583. $6\overline{)342}$

584. $8\overline{)704}$

585. $3\overline{)96}$

586. $4\overline{)192}$

587. $2\overline{)188}$

588. $3\overline{)177}$

589. $4\overline{)308}$

590. $6\overline{)492}$

591. $5\overline{)440}$

592. $10\overline{)770}$

593. $7\overline{)539}$

594. $9\overline{)765}$

595. $4\overline{)116}$

596. $2\overline{)4}$

597. $9\overline{)612}$

598. $4\overline{)8}$

599. $8\overline{)32}$

600. $7\overline{)273}$

601. $5\overline{)410}$

602. $7\overline{)175}$

603. $10\overline{)20}$

604. $9\overline{)450}$

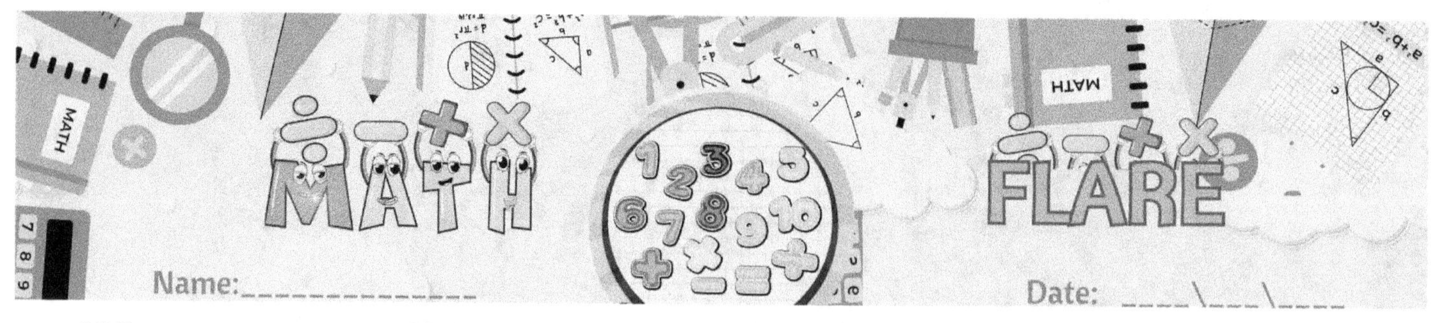

605.

$$9\overline{)171}$$

606.

$$2\overline{)18}$$

607.

$$10\overline{)30}$$

608.

$$1\overline{)42}$$

609.

$$9\overline{)36}$$

610.

$$10\overline{)390}$$

611.

$$1\overline{)100}$$

612.

$$4\overline{)64}$$

613.

$$3\overline{)87}$$

614.

$$10\overline{)540}$$

615.

$$5\overline{)90}$$

616.

$$2\overline{)166}$$

617.

$$3\overline{)210}$$

618.

$$9\overline{)369}$$

619.

$$9\overline{)108}$$

620.

$$2\overline{)8}$$

Name:_____________________   Date: _______________

621.

2)180

622.

7)210

623.

10)360

624.

2)126

625.

5)55

626.

8)576

627.

9)747

628.

10)380

629.

3)192

630.

3)186

631.

9)702

632.

10)220

633.

3)54

634.

3)174

635.

5)455

636.

9)315

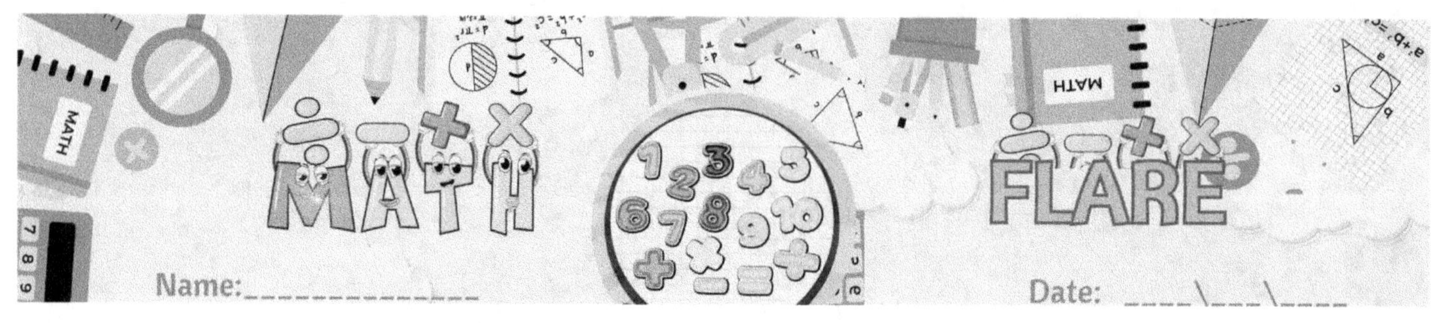

637.

$1\overline{)17}$

638.

$9\overline{)873}$

639.

$4\overline{)256}$

640.

$4\overline{)216}$

641.

$4\overline{)140}$

642.

$10\overline{)350}$

643.

$8\overline{)368}$

644.

$3\overline{)90}$

645.

$9\overline{)468}$

646.

$2\overline{)68}$

647.

$4\overline{)344}$

648.

$5\overline{)415}$

649.

$9\overline{)486}$

650.

$8\overline{)624}$

651.

$6\overline{)162}$

652.

$4\overline{)224}$

653.

3)114

654.

2)60

655.

5)315

656.

3)270

657.

5)85

658.

3)213

659.

9)18

660.

7)378

661.

6)234

662.

2)174

663.

7)336

664.

5)210

665.

6)582

666.

10)910

667.

10)370

668.

4)300

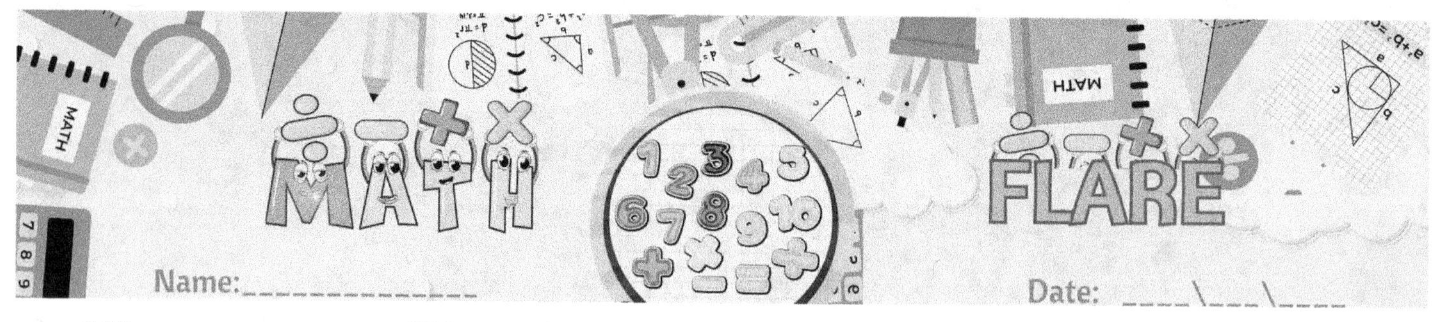

669.

$$3\overline{)9}$$

670.

$$5\overline{)355}$$

671.

$$6\overline{)132}$$

672.

$$6\overline{)414}$$

673.

$$5\overline{)245}$$

674.

$$9\overline{)459}$$

675.

$$4\overline{)40}$$

676.

$$7\overline{)553}$$

677.

$$1\overline{)86}$$

678.

$$3\overline{)66}$$

679.

$$7\overline{)686}$$

680.

$$2\overline{)168}$$

681.

$$4\overline{)184}$$

682.

$$8\overline{)408}$$

683.

$$3\overline{)189}$$

684.

$$2\overline{)96}$$

685.

$6 \overline{)558}$

686.

$1 \overline{)31}$

687.

$8 \overline{)344}$

688.

$5 \overline{)80}$

689.

$6 \overline{)588}$

690.

$2 \overline{)92}$

691.

$1 \overline{)45}$

692.

$4 \overline{)76}$

693.

$4 \overline{)172}$

694.

$5 \overline{)25}$

695.

$4 \overline{)176}$

696.

$6 \overline{)402}$

697.

$9 \overline{)828}$

698.

$5 \overline{)425}$

699.

$7 \overline{)91}$

700.

$9 \overline{)630}$

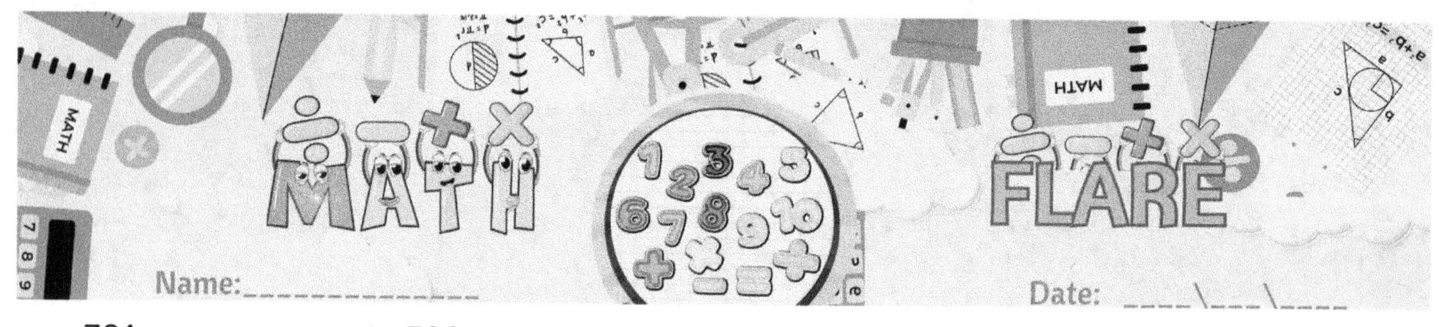

701.

$$8\overline{)592}$$

702.

$$1\overline{)84}$$

703.

$$8\overline{)400}$$

704.

$$8\overline{)712}$$

705.

$$3\overline{)6}$$

706.

$$10\overline{)420}$$

707.

$$4\overline{)144}$$

708.

$$6\overline{)324}$$

709.

$$9\overline{)261}$$

710.

$$6\overline{)156}$$

711.

$$8\overline{)728}$$

712.

$$6\overline{)354}$$

713.

$$5\overline{)295}$$

714.

$$3\overline{)264}$$

715.

$$10\overline{)800}$$

716.

$$9\overline{)207}$$

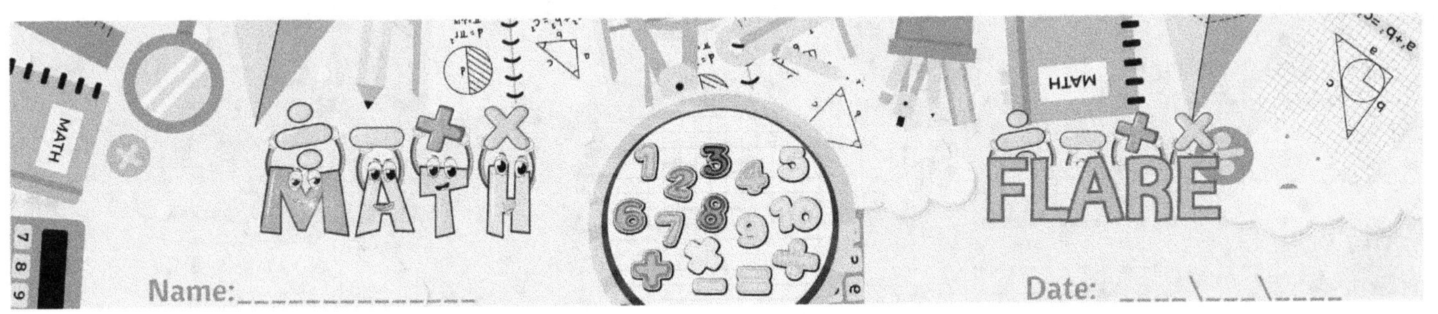

717.

7)525

718.

4)164

719.

4)136

720.

4)96

721.

6)294

722.

2)104

723.

8)512

724.

6)426

725.

3)99

726.

2)114

727.

5)235

728.

1)99

729.

9)513

730.

5)305

731.

3)237

732.

4)28

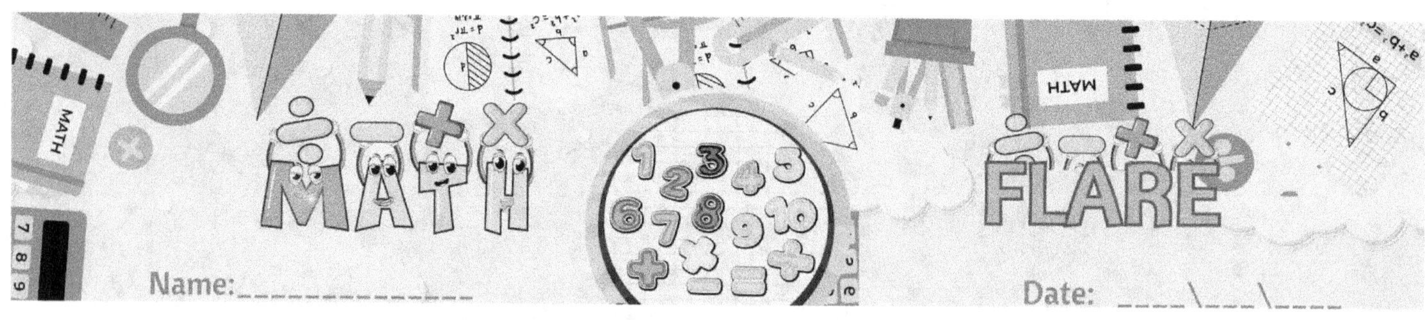

Long Division: Remainders

Find the quotient.

733.

10$\overline{)618}$

734.

9$\overline{)743}$

735.

9$\overline{)453}$

736.

6$\overline{)185}$

737.

16$\overline{)488}$

738.

8$\overline{)991}$

739.

$4\overline{)987}$

740.

$2\overline{)303}$

741.

$16\overline{)923}$

742.

$2\overline{)801}$

743.

$4\overline{)104}$

744.

$8\overline{)767}$

745.

6)616

746.

12)581

747.

2)112

748.

17)640

749.

13)540

750.

15)680

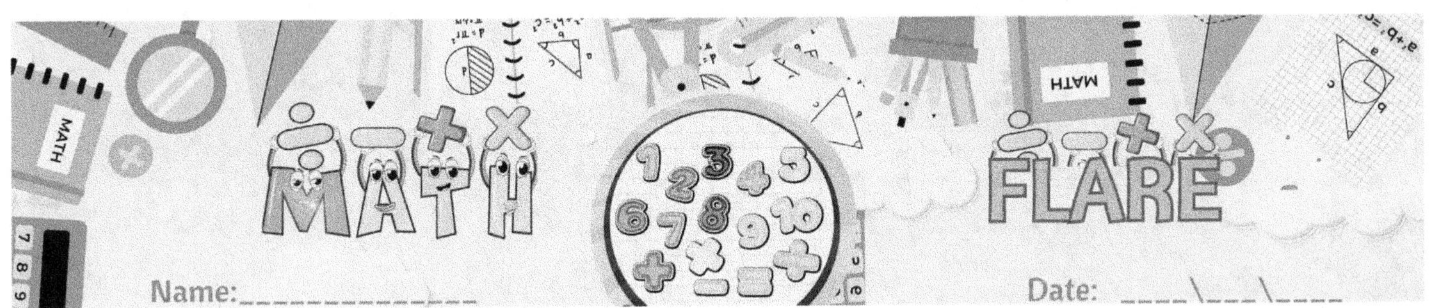

751.

5) 689

752.

14) 857

753.

12) 806

754.

4) 717

755.

6) 308

756.

13) 271

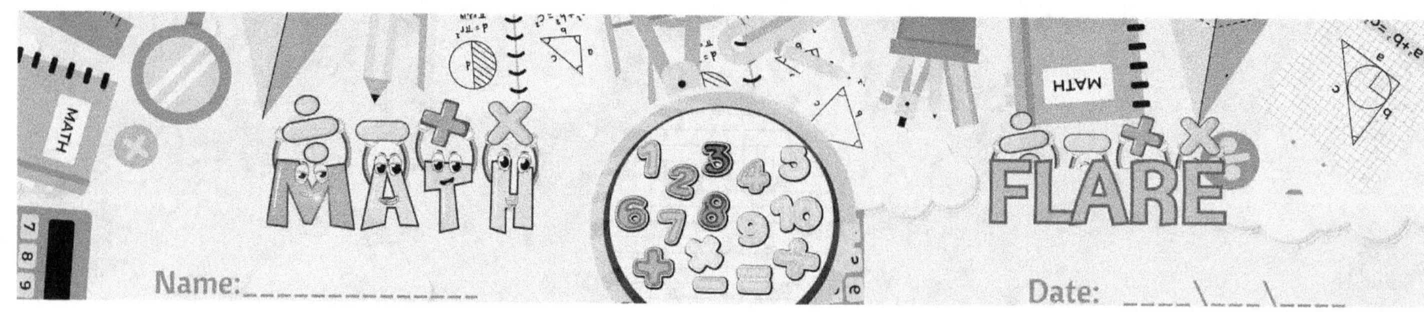

757.

$$16\overline{)590}$$

758.

$$19\overline{)351}$$

759.

$$18\overline{)346}$$

760.

$$10\overline{)631}$$

761.

$$9\overline{)751}$$

762.

$$5\overline{)857}$$

763.

12)892

764.

10)264

765.

4)280

766.

9)841

767.

11)498

768.

15)411

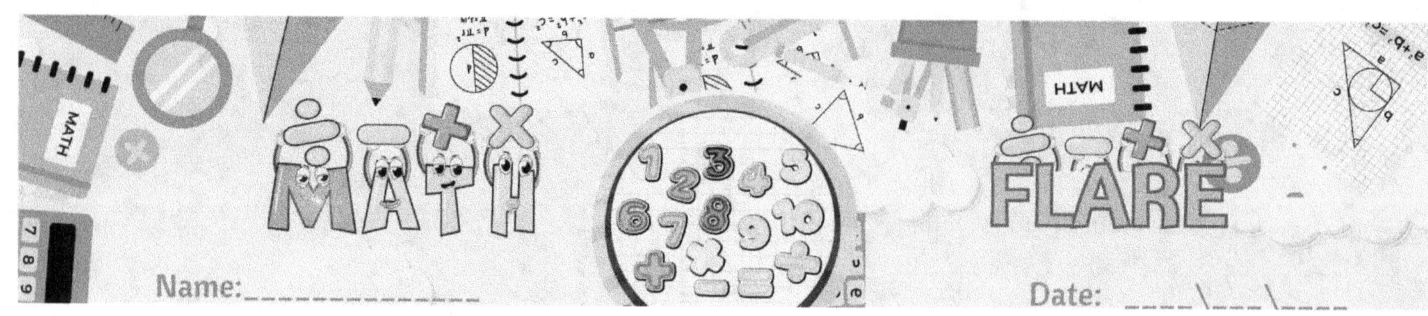

769.

$$4\overline{)959}$$

770.

$$10\overline{)299}$$

771.

$$14\overline{)503}$$

772.

$$9\overline{)169}$$

773.

$$18\overline{)124}$$

774.

$$6\overline{)986}$$

775.

14)‾750‾

776.

13)‾626‾

777.

6)‾112‾

778.

6)‾985‾

779.

14)‾412‾

780.

6)‾788‾

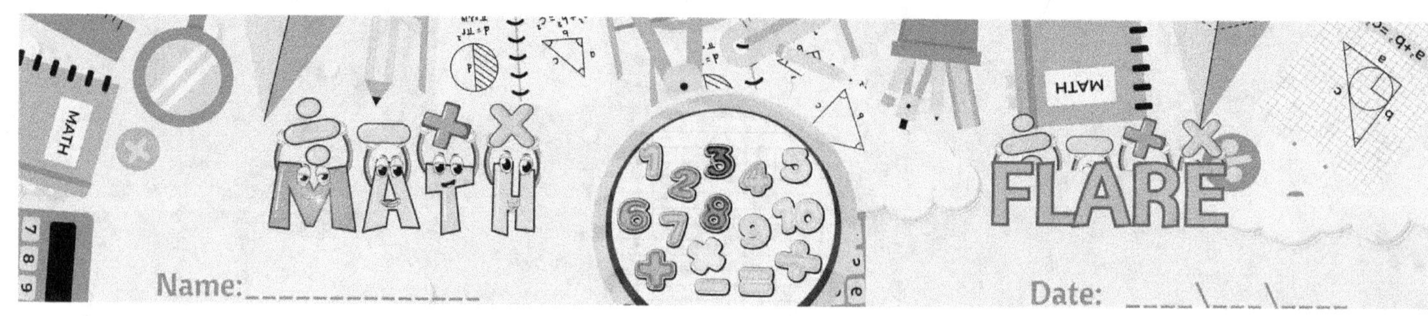

781.

$7\overline{)440}$

782.

$4\overline{)912}$

783.

$17\overline{)440}$

784.

$2\overline{)272}$

785.

$12\overline{)506}$

786.

$5\overline{)964}$

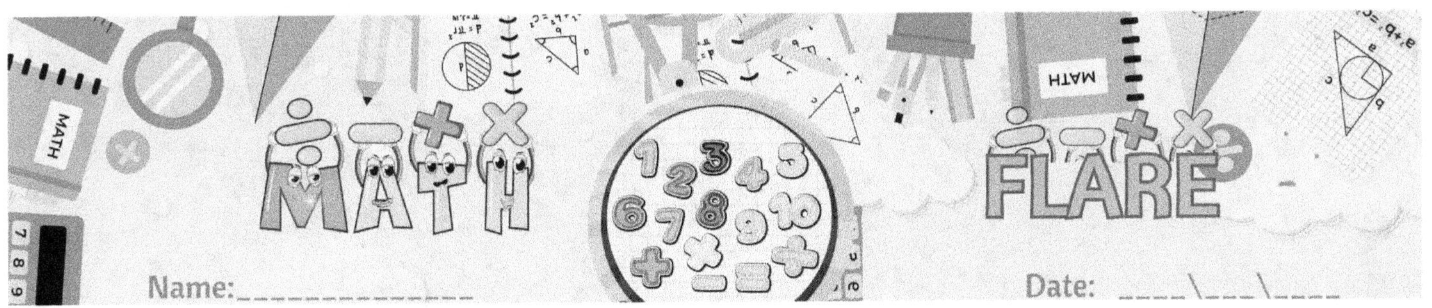

787.

$$5 \overline{)699}$$

788.

$$4 \overline{)993}$$

789.

$$10 \overline{)396}$$

790.

$$20 \overline{)234}$$

791.

$$19 \overline{)621}$$

792.

$$11 \overline{)735}$$

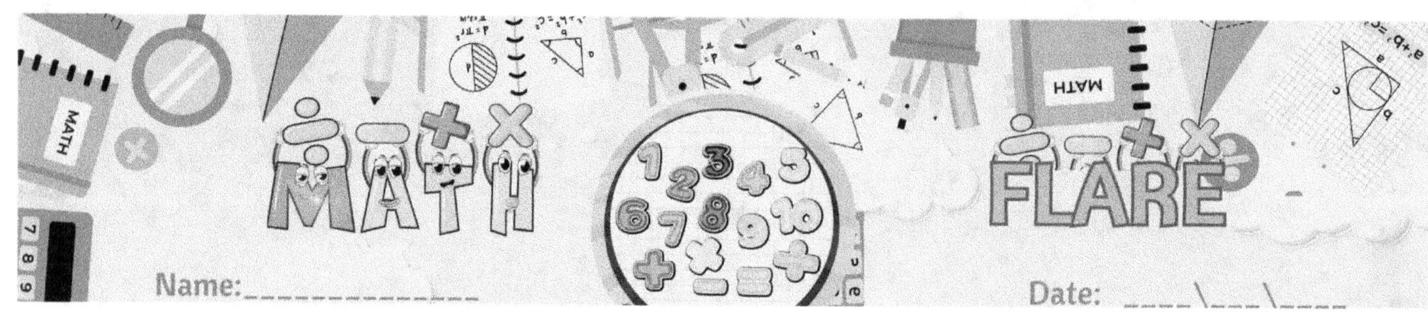

793.

$$6\overline{)592}$$

794.

$$6\overline{)431}$$

795.

$$4\overline{)579}$$

796.

$$7\overline{)442}$$

797.

$$2\overline{)431}$$

798.

$$5\overline{)159}$$

799.

$$20 \overline{)762}$$

800.

$$6 \overline{)994}$$

801.

$$19 \overline{)737}$$

802.

$$5 \overline{)787}$$

803.

$$10 \overline{)750}$$

804.

$$18 \overline{)942}$$

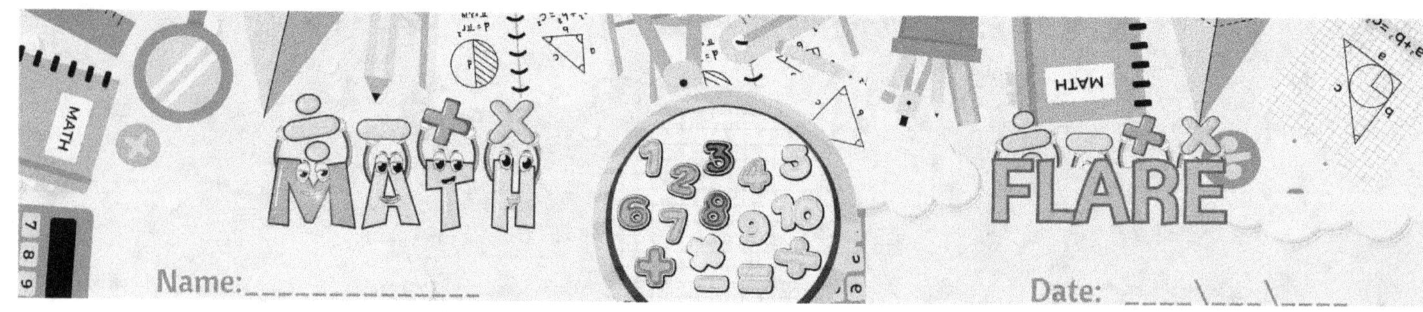

805.

18)289

806.

18)926

807.

16)565

808.

9)677

809.

9)596

810.

5)596

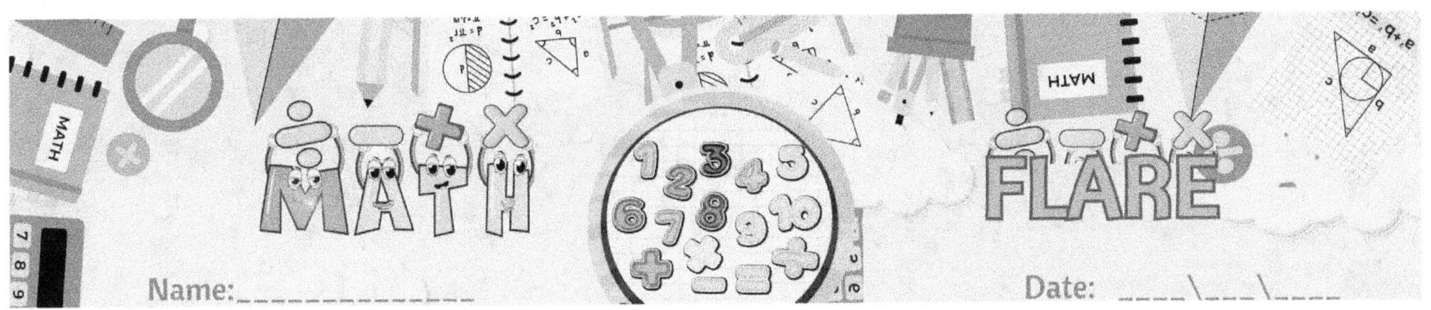

811.

$$19\overline{)495}$$

812.

$$8\overline{)545}$$

813.

$$14\overline{)254}$$

814.

$$14\overline{)794}$$

815.

$$16\overline{)172}$$

816.

$$8\overline{)414}$$

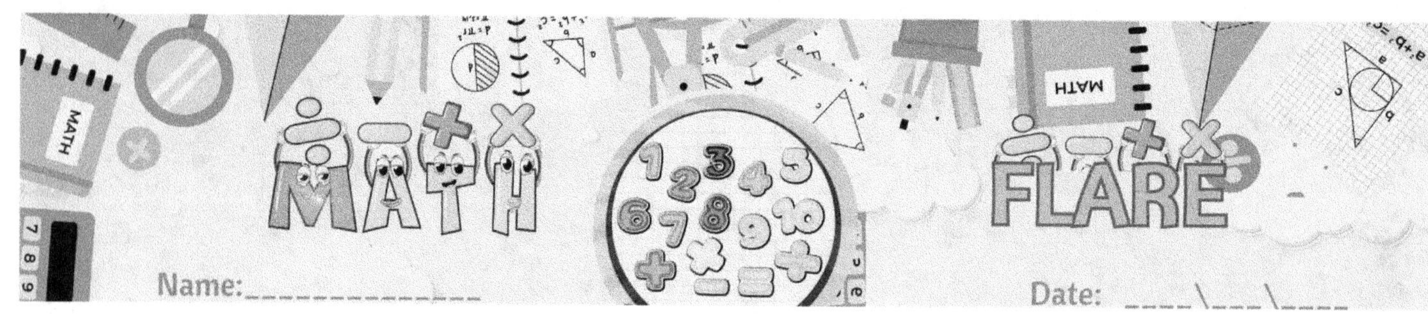

817.

$$19\overline{)527}$$

818.

$$13\overline{)344}$$

819.

$$12\overline{)282}$$

820.

$$4\overline{)812}$$

821.

$$11\overline{)357}$$

822.

$$13\overline{)125}$$

ANSWERS

Page 1:   Basic Division

1. 11	2. 19	3. 13	4. 14	5. 12	6. 6	7. 9	8. 11
9. 16	10. 4	11. 2	12. 7	13. 14	14. 14	15. 16	16. 10
17. 6	18. 2	19. 15	20. 11	21. 18	22. 15	23. 3	24. 1
25. 3	26. 3	27. 15	28. 14	29. 11	30. 14	31. 5	32. 17
33. 17	34. 14	35. 11	36. 1	37. 10	38. 5	39. 2	40. 13
41. 15	42. 2	43. 9	44. 10	45. 12	46. 12	47. 8	48. 20
49. 20	50. 6	51. 17	52. 6	53. 19	54. 7	55. 20	56. 13
57. 19	58. 5	59. 10	60. 8	61. 6	62. 2	63. 9	64. 1
65. 6	66. 4	67. 18	68. 19	69. 14	70. 16	71. 15	72. 4
73. 19	74. 7	75. 11	76. 1	77. 2	78. 11	79. 8	80. 4
81. 17	82. 15	83. 4	84. 12	85. 13	86. 2	87. 16	88. 18
89. 4	90. 19	91. 17	92. 3	93. 15	94. 16	95. 13	96. 12
97. 17	98. 16	99. 13	100. 12	101. 8	102. 19	103. 10	104. 8
105. 12	106. 15	107. 15	108. 16	109. 6	110. 1	111. 17	112. 14
113. 17	114. 9	115. 9	116. 14	117. 13	118. 1	119. 18	120. 20
121. 7	122. 4	123. 10	124. 9	125. 7	126. 7	127. 10	128. 6
129. 9	130. 12	131. 6	132. 13	133. 8	134. 10	135. 3	136. 20
137. 10	138. 14	139. 4	140. 8	141. 18	142. 11	143. 11	144. 5

Page 10: Basic Division

145. 17   146. 6   147. 12   148. 16   149. 14   150. 7   151. 4
152. 9   153. 13   154. 17   155. 4   156. 4   157. 14   158. 2
159. 16   160. 17   161. 6   162. 19   163. 3   164. 10   165. 18
166. 10   167. 5   168. 5   169. 17   170. 20   171. 3   172. 19
173. 1   174. 3   175. 2   176. 13   177. 3   178. 9   179. 19
180. 3   181. 11   182. 7   183. 5   184. 1   185. 8   186. 16
187. 3   188. 6   189. 5   190. 14   191. 3   192. 12   193. 18
194. 12   195. 3   196. 12   197. 9   198. 7   199. 17   200. 15
201. 6   202. 14   203. 20   204. 13   205. 6   206. 6   207. 7
208. 6   209. 4   210. 4   211. 8   212. 14   213. 15   214. 6
215. 13   216. 18   217. 15   218. 16   219. 19   220. 7   221. 8
222. 9   223. 5   224. 10   225. 10   226. 15   227. 10   228. 10
229. 12   230. 8   231. 16   232. 1   233. 8   234. 15   235. 15
236. 20   237. 19   238. 12   239. 2   240. 1   241. 5   242. 9
243. 18   244. 2   245. 10   246. 16   247. 4   248. 10   249. 18
250. 11   251. 16   252. 9   253. 13   254. 6   255. 5   256. 14
257. 18   258. 10   259. 5   260. 7   261. 12   262. 7   263. 2
264. 4   265. 18   266. 11   267. 2   268. 9   269. 18   270. 5
271. 11   272. 20   273. 1   274. 12   275. 19   276. 12   277. 15
278. 19   279. 20   280. 11   281. 13   282. 17   283. 18   284. 4

285. 11	286. 2	287. 14	288. 8	289. 20	290. 2	291. 17
292. 19	293. 8	294. 18	295. 9	296. 3	297. 16	298. 13
299. 1	300. 19	301. 11	302. 5	303. 7	304. 15	305. 11
306. 2	307. 8	308. 20	309. 1	310. 15	311. 8	312. 17
313. 4	314. 1	315. 16	316. 19	317. 15	318. 10	319. 8
320. 7	321. 17	322. 4	323. 6	324. 1	325. 14	326. 9
327. 2	328. 13	329. 3	330. 20	331. 11	332. 20	333. 13
334. 17	335. 9	336. 16				

Page 22:   Long Division

337. 37	338. 90	339. 67	340. 39	341. 10	342. 72	343. 62
344. 80	345. 22	346. 20	347. 31	348. 79	349. 69	350. 95
351. 89	352. 26	353. 95	354. 21	355. 86	356. 77	357. 43
358. 87	359. 25	360. 20	361. 82	362. 8	363. 32	364. 83
365. 82	366. 32	367. 54	368. 86	369. 60	370. 2	371. 81
372. 73	373. 8	374. 83	375. 98	376. 31	377. 79	378. 99
379. 62	380. 45	381. 73	382. 49	383. 39	384. 5	385. 22
386. 95	387. 64	388. 8	389. 23	390. 85	391. 70	392. 88
393. 39	394. 29	395. 41	396. 43	397. 51	398. 12	399. 69
400. 52	401. 67	402. 96	403. 9	404. 45	405. 68	406. 49
407. 71	408. 87	409. 31	410. 89	411. 69	412. 50	413. 47
414. 90	415. 60	416. 48	417. 36	418. 56	419. 48	420. 49

421. 81   422. 14   423. 43   424. 95   425. 93   426. 94   427. 10

428. 91   429. 60   430. 57   431. 96   432. 3   433. 34   434. 3

435. 97   436. 19   437. 53   438. 34   439. 33   440. 66   441. 45

442. 1   443. 81   444. 88   445. 61   446. 80   447. 62   448. 86

449. 28   450. 72   451. 19   452. 68   453. 66   454. 18   455. 35

456. 61   457. 38   458. 55   459. 1   460. 22   461. 51   462. 65

463. 71   464. 94   465. 62   466. 2   467. 57   468. 8   469. 64

470. 66   471. 87   472. 15   473. 83   474. 39   475. 5   476. 61

477. 66   478. 85   479. 7   480. 17   481. 84   482. 65   483. 41

484. 53   485. 7   486. 27   487. 21   488. 70   489. 44   490. 92

491. 56   492. 66   493. 98   494. 62   495. 81   496. 75   497. 38

498. 82   499. 2   500. 21   501. 41   502. 31   503. 39   504. 87

505. 11   506. 95   507. 39   508. 99   509. 82   510. 80   511. 56

512. 98   513. 58   514. 46   515. 11   516. 69   517. 78   518. 68

519. 70   520. 93   521. 62   522. 40   523. 92   524. 62   525. 22

526. 82   527. 13   528. 91   529. 25   530. 44   531. 55   532. 78

533. 95   534. 76   535. 76   536. 41

Page 34: Long Division

537. 36   538. 44   539. 62   540. 5   541. 1   542. 97   543. 69

544. 89   545. 54   546. 77   547. 3   548. 82   549. 12   550. 68

551. 21   552. 64   553. 78   554. 7   555. 18   556. 47   557. 56

558. 89   559. 72   560. 30   561. 29   562. 55   563. 89   564. 42

565. 17   566. 76   567. 13   568. 80   569. 66   570. 98   571. 24

572. 74   573. 12   574. 36   575. 45   576. 99   577. 15   578. 17

579. 22   580. 72   581. 39   582. 11   583. 57   584. 88   585. 32

586. 48   587. 94   588. 59   589. 77   590. 82   591. 88   592. 77

593. 77   594. 85   595. 29   596. 2   597. 68   598. 2   599. 4

600. 39   601. 82   602. 25   603. 2   604. 50   605. 19   606. 9

607. 3   608. 42   609. 4   610. 39   611. 100   612. 16   613. 29

614. 54   615. 18   616. 83   617. 70   618. 41   619. 12   620. 4

621. 90   622. 30   623. 36   624. 63   625. 11   626. 72   627. 83

628. 38   629. 64   630. 62   631. 78   632. 22   633. 18   634. 58

635. 91   636. 35   637. 17   638. 97   639. 64   640. 54   641. 35

642. 35   643. 46   644. 30   645. 52   646. 34   647. 86   648. 83

649. 54   650. 78   651. 27   652. 56   653. 38   654. 30   655. 63

656. 90   657. 17   658. 71   659. 2   660. 54   661. 39   662. 87

663. 48   664. 42   665. 97   666. 91   667. 37   668. 75   669. 3

670. 71   671. 22   672. 69   673. 49   674. 51   675. 10   676. 79

677. 86   678. 22   679. 98   680. 84   681. 46   682. 51   683. 63

684. 48   685. 93   686. 31   687. 43   688. 16   689. 98   690. 46

691. 45   692. 19   693. 43   694. 5   695. 44   696. 67   697. 92

698. 85   699. 13   700. 70   701. 74   702. 84   703. 50   704. 89

705. 2 706. 42 707. 36 708. 54 709. 29 710. 26 711. 91

712. 59 713. 59 714. 88 715. 80 716. 23 717. 75 718. 41

719. 34 720. 24 721. 49 722. 52 723. 64 724. 71 725. 33

726. 57 727. 47 728. 99 729. 57 730. 61 731. 79 732. 7

Page 47: Long Division: Remainders

733. 61 R8 734. 82 R5 735. 50 R3 736. 30 R5 737. 30 R8

738. 123 R7 739. 246 R3 740. 151 R1 741. 57 R11 742. 400 R1

743. 26 R0 744. 95 R7 745. 102 R4 746. 48 R5 747. 56 R0

748. 37 R11 749. 41 R7 750. 45 R5 751. 137 R4 752. 61 R3

753. 67 R2 754. 179 R1 755. 51 R2 756. 20 R11 757. 36 R14

758. 18 R9 759. 19 R4 760. 63 R1 761. 83 R4 762. 171 R2

763. 74 R4 764. 26 R4 765. 70 R0 766. 93 R4 767. 45 R3

768. 27 R6 769. 239 R3 770. 29 R9 771. 35 R13 772. 18 R7

773. 6 R16 774. 164 R2 775. 53 R8 776. 48 R2 777. 18 R4

778. 164 R1 779. 29 R6 780. 131 R2 781. 62 R6 782. 228 R0

783. 25 R15 784. 136 R0 785. 42 R2 786. 192 R4 787. 139 R4

788. 248 R1 789. 39 R6 790. 11 R14 791. 32 R13 792. 66 R9

793. 98 R4 794. 71 R5 795. 144 R3 796. 63 R1 797. 215 R1

798. 31 R4 799. 38 R2 800. 165 R4 801. 38 R15 802. 157 R2

803. 75 R0 804. 52 R6 805. 16 R1 806. 51 R8 807. 35 R5

808. 75 R2 809. 66 R2 810. 119 R1 811. 26 R1 812. 68 R1

813. 18 R2   814. 56 R10   815. 10 R12   816. 51 R6   817. 27 R14

818. 26 R6   819. 23 R6   820. 203 R0   821. 32 R5   822. 9 R8